Original title:
Zesty Tunes Inside the Dragon Haul

Author: Sabrina Sarvik
ISBN HARDBACK: 978-1-80559-359-1
ISBN PAPERBACK: 978-1-80559-858-9

Echoing Sagas of the Unyielding

In valleys deep where shadows play,
The whispers of the past hold sway.
Through ancient trees, the stories breathe,
Of courage found and hearts that cleave.

Each echo carries strength anew,
From battles fought and foes they slew.
In every leaf a tale unfolds,
Of heroes brave and legends bold.

With every step on time-worn ground,
The pulse of history resounds.
Through trials faced and burdens borne,
The spirit's fire is never worn.

Resilience shines in darkest night,
A beacon, fierce and burning bright.
Through storms that rage and winds that wail,
The unyielding heart will never pale.

So gather 'round and listen well,
To sagas rich that time will tell.
For in these tales, we find our place,
In whispered dreams and fierce embrace.

Flames Reflecting Twilight's Song

As dusk descends and firelight glows,
The world transforms, the quiet flows.
In golden hues, the day surrenders,
While whispers of the night then mender.

With every crackle, stories weave,
Of moonlit nights that all believe.
The embers dance with shadows tall,
In perfect grace, they rise and fall.

Among the stars, a melody wakes,
Twilight's song as daylight breaks.
In gentle sighs, the whispers blend,
A symphony that has no end.

The flames reflect the dreams we chase,
In every flicker, a warm embrace.
With hearts aligned, we gather near,
To share our hopes, to calm our fear.

So let the night unfold its grace,
With each bright flame, a sacred space.
For in this moment, we belong,
Together in twilight's tender song.

Nightfall Overtures of the Winged One

Beneath the fading sun's soft sigh,
Whispers of wings begin to rise.
Stars awaken, painting the sky,
Night unveils its velvet guise.

A hush descends, the world stands still,
Moonlight dances on the sea.
Echoes of night, a gentle thrill,
Calling forth the wild and free.

From shadows deep, soft forms take flight,
Glimmers of hope, in dusky glow.
As symphonies weave through the night,
The winged one sings, a heart aglow.

In every note, a story told,
Of dreams that linger in the dark.
Secrets of dawn, in silver and gold,
Freed by the sound of a soul's spark.

So let the night cradle your fears,
For twilight's magic holds you tight.
In every heartbeat, joy appears,
As the winged one takes to flight.

Celebrations from the Hidden Depths

In caverns where the silence sleeps,
Mysteries shimmer in gloaming light.
Creatures of the night, their secret keeps,
Under the surface, dreams take flight.

Bubbles rise from the ocean floor,
Tales of old in harmony swell.
Echoes of joy, they sing and soar,
Celebrations hidden, weaving a spell.

The tides of time embrace the night,
As laughter bubbles up from below.
Gifts of the sea, in pure delight,
Illuminate the path we'll go.

Stars reflect on waves that dance,
Lighting up the depths with grace.
In every swell lies a fleeting chance,
To join the merry tide's embrace.

So dive in deep, where secrets gleam,
And let the currents guide your way.
In hidden depths, unfold the dream,
For every night births a brand-new day.

Chiming of the Crystal Scales

In forests where the shadows play,
A melody of twinkling sound.
Crystal scales in twilight sway,
Their shimmering song can astound.

Each note a whisper from the trees,
Caught in the breeze, they swirl and gleam.
A chorus born from ancient seas,
Echoes of a long-lost dream.

Fragments of light spin and flow,
As harmony drifts through the night.
Guided by stars' gentle glow,
Chiming echoes set our hearts alight.

With each soft chime, a tale is spun,
Of creatures who dance in the dark.
A world of wonder, newly begun,
Where passion ignites every spark.

So listen close to the evening's song,
For crystal scales hold tales untold.
In their rhythms, we all belong,
A treasure of magic, pure and bold.

The Heartbeat of Enchanted Flames

In the twilight's warm embrace,
A flickering glow begins to pulse.
Dancing shadows in a mystic space,
Where embers stir and dreams convulse.

Winds whisper tales of fire's heart,
As sparks ignite the night profound.
In every flame, a world apart,
A tapestry of love unbound.

Feel the rhythm, the glowing beat,
The heartbeat of a timeless lore.
Each flicker sings, embracing heat,
A symphony from ages yore.

Light the night with stories bright,
As flames entwine with souls of old.
In this dance, all fears take flight,
In the warmth of magic, hearts unfold.

So gather close as shadows play,
Let the flames weave their vibrant dreams.
For in their bliss, we find our way,
In the heartbeat of enchanted themes.

Resounding Joy in the Ashen Grove

In the grove where shadows dance,
Whispers of laughter take their chance.
Beneath the boughs where embers glow,
Resounding joy begins to flow.

Leaves drift softly, painted gold,
Stories of warmth and love retold.
Branches sway, as if in song,
Embracing all who drift along.

Laughter echoes, soft and clear,
Filling hearts, dispelling fear.
In every rustle, life anew,
Hope emerges, strong and true.

Endless dreams in twilight's hue,
Light the path for me and you.
Under stars that gently gleam,
Together we can chase the dream.

In ashen grove, our spirits soar,
Finding joy forevermore.
With every beat, the world ignites,
In unity, our hearts take flight.

The Sunset Serenade of Firebreath

When day departs in fiery blaze,
The sky ignites in golden rays.
A serenade of colors dance,
As shadows whisper sweet romance.

Crimson clouds and amber skies,
A world transformed before our eyes.
The sun dips low with a final breath,
Igniting dreams, defying death.

Softly now, the night begins,
With gentle hums, the silence spins.
Each twinkle sparkles, bright and near,
A promise kept, forever clear.

In this twilight, warmth surrounds,
The heartbeat of the earth resounds.
With every note that nature weaves,
We mend our souls, embrace believes.

So let the fire breathe its song,
For in this place, we all belong.
Together, as the stars arise,
We find our strength beneath the skies.

Trail of Mirth in the Lair's Heart

In the depths where secrets hide,
Mirthful whispers softly glide.
Upon the trail of laughter's trace,
We find the heart of hidden grace.

Through twisted roots and midnight air,
We dance through shadows, free from care.
With every step, the echoes rise,
A melody beneath the skies.

In the lair where shadows play,
We'll sing our fears and doubts away.
Embraced by warmth of friendship's light,
Together we can chase the night.

With each heartbeat, joy expands,
Uniting all with gentle hands.
In laughter's glow, our spirits blend,
On this trail, there is no end.

So follow me to where dreams start,
In the lair's embrace, we find our heart.
Through every moment, let us roam,
For in this mirth, we're always home.

Songs of Luminescent Echoes

In the night, the echoes sing,
Of luminescence, hope they bring.
Through the mist, they weave and flow,
A symphony of dreams that glow.

Stars align in cosmic play,
Guiding us along the way.
Soft whispers of the universe,
In every note, the world converses.

With gentle harmonies that rise,
We find our truth beneath the skies.
In every shimmer, a tale unfolds,
Of love and laughter, brave and bold.

Through valleys deep and mountains high,
The songs remind us to reach for the sky.
In the echoes, our spirits soar,
An eternal dance forevermore.

So let us sing till the dawn breaks,
In the luminous trail that wakes.
With echoes, we will find our place,
In the songs that time can't erase.

Scale and Melody: A Dragon's Refrain

In the caverns deep and wide,
The dragon's heart begins to glide.
With scales that shimmer, flash, and gleam,
It dances to a timeless dream.

A melody of fire and grace,
Echoing through space and place.
Wings unfurled in twilight's glow,
Its spirit sings, a vibrant flow.

Each note a spark, each chord a flame,
In the night, it calls its name.
A symphony of ancient skies,
That lingers long after it flies.

In solitude, it finds its tune,
Beneath the watchful, silver moon.
A swirling breeze, a whispered song,
Reminding us where we belong.

So gather round, let stories soar,
Of dragons' hearts and legends' lore.
In scale and melody entwined,
A lasting magic, undefined.

Firelight and Wishes: A Harmonious Venture

By the fire where shadows play,
Wishes dance and dreams may stay.
With flickering flames, hope ignites,
A tapestry of starry nights.

Laughter mingles with the glow,
As secrets whispered softly flow.
Each spark a wish cast high above,
In harmony, we share our love.

The warmth wraps round like a cloak,
In every heart, a tender joke.
With every flicker, stories bloom,
In firelight's embrace, dispelling gloom.

We gather close and feel the cheer,
A bond that time cannot smear.
Through flames and laughter, we shall soar,
In wishes bright, forevermore.

So raise your voice and sing out loud,
In every heart, a vibrant crowd.
With firelight and wishes bright,
We venture forth into the night.

Ballads beneath the Winged Horizon

Beneath the sky where eagles soar,
A ballad sings forevermore.
With every breeze, a story told,
Of legends lost and dreams of old.

The horizon gleams with colors bright,
As day melts softly into night.
In whispered tones, the world will sway,
To melodies of night and day.

From mountain high to valley low,
The songs of life begin to flow.
In harmony with nature's grace,
Each note a step in time and space.

With every heartbeat, every sound,
The pulse of dreams, forever bound.
In ballads woven tight with care,
A tapestry of love to share.

So heed the calls that softly rise,
As dusk embraces painted skies.
In every note, we find our place,
Beneath the winged horizon's grace.

Flame-Kissed Harmonies of Old

In a realm where shadows play,
Flame-kissed harmonies hold sway.
Echoes of the past resound,
In every corner, magic found.

With every flicker, stories blend,
Of hero's journey, love, and friend.
A symphony of heart and soul,
Two worlds unite to make us whole.

The embers glow, a guiding light,
As melodies take sacred flight.
In dusk's embrace, we weave our dreams,
In every heart, a spark that gleams.

Together, we will sing our song,
Through flame and shadow, we belong.
Harmonies of ages spun,
We share the dance, we are all one.

So gather close, and let it be,
In every sound, we find the key.
To flame-kissed truths, we raise the voice,
In ancient tales, we rejoice.

Guitar of the Celestial Being

Strings that hum a cosmic tune,
Whispers from the silver moon.
Harmony of the starry night,
Playing dreams in purest light.

In the silence, echoes play,
Melodies that drift away.
Celestial chords in graceful dance,
Binding time in a trance.

Fingers weave the astral sound,
Notes like stardust all around.
A symphony beyond the far,
The heart of a celestial star.

Resonant waves in endless space,
Every note a warm embrace.
Guitar of light, in shadows cast,
Sings of futures, echoes past.

Enigma of the Draconic Symphony

In the night, shadows creep,
Where ancient legends sleep.
A dragon's roar, a haunting sound,
Mysteries that whirl around.

Fires dance in the moonlit sky,
As the notes take to the high.
Wings unfurl with thunder's might,
In the heart of endless night.

Woven tales of battles fought,
In every melody, wisdom sought.
The symphony of earth and sky,
Calling forth the years gone by.

Chords that rumble, deep and low,
Secrets in the flames that glow.
A enigma wrapped in sound,
In the dragon's heart, we're bound.

Ballad Beyond the Abyss

Beyond the edge, where shadows dwell,
A ballad weaves its timeless spell.
With whispers soft, the echoes rise,
Guiding lost souls through darkened skies.

In the depths, where silence sings,
Hope emerges on fragile wings.
A tapestry of light and gloom,
Bears witness to forgotten doom.

Each note a tear, a lover's sigh,
In the void, where dreams could die.
Yet melodies of distant shores,
Resonate behind closed doors.

From shadows deep, a flame ignites,
A courage born from starry nights.
In the abyss, one finds their song,
A ballad true where hearts belong.

Songs of the Embered Odyssey

Winds of fate on fiery trails,
Songs of journeys fill the sails.
Every ember tells a tale,
Of adventures fierce and frail.

In the glow of twilight's hue,
Echoes of the brave ring true.
A chorus rising with the dawn,
In every heart, a spark is drawn.

Shadows dance around the flame,
Each note whispers a name.
Through the years in twilight's grace,
The journey finds its rightful place.

With courage burning in our chests,
We face the trials and the tests.
Embered songs that guide our way,
In the odyssey, we find our stay.

Lullabies of the Fiery Beast

In the night, whispers flow,
Underneath the crimson glow.
Softly sings the beast of fire,
Crackling dreams of pure desire.

Around the embers, shadows dance,
Echoes hold a fleeting chance.
As the stars begin to fade,
Night's embrace will not evade.

With wings that span the starlit skies,
A lullaby of ancient cries.
In the warmth of glowing light,
Sleep now drifts into the night.

Fireflies weave a bright ballet,
Guiding dreams that drift away.
In the heart of wild, untamed,
The lullabies are softly named.

Hear the whispers, soft and clear,
In the night, the beast is near.
Close your eyes, let shadows roam,
In this fire, you find your home.

Symphony of the Scales and Stars

A melody of crested waves,
In the night, where silence saves.
Stars above begin to twinkle,
While the scales of dragons crinkle.

Harmonies in the dark abound,
Echoes of a thundering sound.
Each note dances, fluttering light,
Crafting a dream within the night.

A tapestry of dusk and dawn,
Woven threads of night till morn.
Every scale, a story spun,
Underneath the fiery sun.

Listen close, the music sways,
In the heat of ancient days.
A symphony of fire's embrace,
Wings unfold in timeless grace.

In this realm of stars and scales,
Where the nightingale softly wails.
Feel the rhythm pulse and play,
As the world melts softly away.

Ethereal Echoes from the Aether

Whispers drift through the night's dome,
Carried on winds, far from home.
In the aether, secrets twirl,
Invisible threads begin to unfurl.

Echoes pulse in the stillness,
Crafting dreams, a deep thrillness.
Softly calling, a voice so sweet,
Woven songs where shadows meet.

Reflections of a time long past,
In the echoes, memories cast.
Light and dark, interwoven flow,
In each heartbeat, stories grow.

From the aether, visions gleam,
In this lucid, drifting dream.
Dance along the silver thread,
With each note, let spirits spread.

Ethereal whispers guide the way,
Through the night till break of day.
In the silence, find your peace,
Let the echoes never cease.

A Dragon's Harmony: Flames and Dreams

In the depths where shadows play,
Dragons weave their night ballet.
With every breath, a spark ignites,
Painting dreams in vibrant lights.

Flames that flicker, dance, and soar,
Opening wide the ancient door.
In the heart of the fiery crest,
Lies a harmony, a sacred nest.

Dreams take flight on leathery wings,
With every echo, freedom sings.
In the warmth of embers bright,
Dragons cradle the coming night.

Feel the rhythm of their flight,
Through the dark, into the light.
With each beat, a promise gleams,
In the hush, awaken dreams.

A harmony of hopes and fears,
Sung aloud through the passing years.
In the flames, where visions gleam,
Awaken now, embrace the dream.

The Echoing Legend of Shimmering Scales

In depths where whispers weave and twine,
A tale emerges, pure and divine.
Scales that shimmer in moon's soft glow,
Guard secrets of ages, lost in the flow.

Beneath the ripples, legends sing,
Of creatures born from ancient spring.
Their dreams reflect in the tranquil tide,
Where silence and time harmoniously bide.

Each flick of fin, a story retold,
Of valiant hearts, and treasures bold.
In waters dark, they glide with grace,
An echo of life, a timeless embrace.

Yet storms may come and shadows shift,
Testing the scales, a fateful rift.
But through the turmoil, they rise and soar,
Resilient in spirit, forevermore.

For in the heart of the swirling sea,
The legend lives on, wild and free.
An echoing call of shimmering fate,
Awakening dreams, which patiently wait.

Castles in the Air and Fire

High above the clouds they stand,
Castles built by dreamers' hand.
With walls of light and roofs of flame,
Each spire whispers a boundless name.

In twilight's glow, they sway and dance,
A realm of magic, a fleeting chance.
With windows wide, they gaze below,
At lands of shadows, where silence flows.

Fires crackle with tales untold,
Of brave hearts forged, of visions bold.
In every flicker, a story breathes,
Of love and loss, and autumn leaves.

Beneath the stars, their splendor gleams,
A tapestry woven of countless dreams.
Each castle flares, then fades away,
Leaving whispers at the break of day.

Yet in the hearts of those who dare,
The embers burn, bright and rare.
For in the minds where dreams conspire,
Forever dwell, castles of fire.

Verses Among the Flickering Shadows

In twilight's hush, the shadows play,
Verses drift and gently sway.
Whispers woven on the breeze,
A melody that seeks to please.

Dancing lights like stars descend,
Each flicker holds a tale to send.
Ghostly echoes of laughter ring,
From moments past, forever spring.

The path is lit, yet darkly veiled,
By stories lost and hearts impaled.
Amongst the flickers, visions gleam,
Of hopes once bright, a fading dream.

Yet in the gloom, a spark ignites,
A promise found in fleeting nights.
For shadows hold what light cannot,
The verses penned in what we sought.

So gather 'round the dancing flame,
In every pulse, recall a name.
For tales not spoken shall not cease,
Amidst the shadows, we find peace.

Woven Melodies of the Mystic Beasts

In whispered woods where silence reigns,
Mystic beasts roam, free of chains.
With melodies woven in moonlit threads,
Each note a tale of dreams and dreads.

Among the trees, their spirits rise,
With gentle grace beneath starlit skies.
They hum of worlds unseen, unfound,
A chorus of wonders that knows no bounds.

With every rustle, stories unwind,
Of ancient lore and hearts entwined.
In shadows soft, their laughter glows,
A symphony where wildness flows.

From golden fields to mountains high,
Their songs echo, reaching the sky.
Woven melodies dance in the air,
Inviting souls with a silent prayer.

And when the dawn begins to break,
The beasts retreat, the forest aches.
Yet still, their hymns will ever soar,
In every heart, forevermore.

Chords of the Embered Heartstring

In twilight's hush, the heartstrings play,
Soft whispers linger, night meets day.
Fingers dance on warmth and glow,
Embers flicker, love's gentle flow.

With every strum, old tales arise,
A melody woven through the skies.
Fleeting moments, echoes we share,
Bound by the chords of tender care.

Through shadows deep, the music swells,
In secret corners, the story dwells.
A fire's warmth, a lover's sigh,
Together we soar, forever high.

As stars align in the midnight hue,
Notes entwined, they paint the view.
In hearts ablaze, the embers glow,
Each chord a promise, soft and slow.

So let the night envelop us whole,
Ember's flicker, a timeless role.
In strum and beat, we'll find our way,
The chords of love in bright array.

Songs Beneath the Scale-Laden Stars

Underneath a blanket of endless night,
The scale-laden stars twinkle in flight.
Whispers of dreams in the cosmic sea,
Echo the songs of you and me.

With every breath, the cosmos yields,
A symphony sung in moonlit fields.
Across the sky, our wishes soar,
Bound in song, forevermore.

Through silken clouds, we ride the sound,
Notes of the cosmos, easily found.
A serenade from realms afar,
Guides our hearts like a distant star.

In every twinkle, a tale unfolds,
Of ancient love that time beholds.
The universe listens, our voices blend,
In harmony bright, that never ends.

So gather close beneath the night,
We'll sing to the stars, a shared delight.
For each shimmering light we see,
Holds secrets of love in eternity.

Rhythms of the Flickering Firelight

The fire crackles, a heartbeat loud,
In the dance of shadows, we feel so proud.
Rhythms pulse in soft embrace,
Flickering flames, a sacred space.

With every spark that flares to life,
We share our dreams free from strife.
The night ignites with stories bold,
In fire's embrace, we never grow old.

A flicker here, a glow so warm,
Wrapped tight in love, we'll weather any storm.
Through laughter shared and tender sighs,
The rhythms rise to touch the skies.

In whispers soft, the flames conspire,
To weave our tales, to kindle desire.
We gather close, hearts intertwined,
In the flickering light, true love defined.

So let the night draw us in tight,
As we pulse with the rhythms of firelight.
For in the warmth of these bright flames,
Our hearts dance on, forever unscathed.

Serenade of the Winged Behemoth

High above, where the clouds roam free,
The winged behemoth sings to me.
In the twilight's tender embrace,
Its serenade drifts through time and space.

Feathers gleam with the setting sun,
In every note, a journey begun.
Wings expansive, a glorious sight,
Carrying dreams into the night.

Echoing songs of ancient lore,
Tales of the earth, of sea and shore.
With every flap, new worlds ignite,
The behemoth's serenade takes flight.

Through valleys deep and mountains high,
It carries voices through azure sky.
In haunting tones, we feel our part,
The winged giant sings to the heart.

So listen closely, let your spirit soar,
In the serenade, find solace and more.
As twilight fades and stars emerge,
The winged behemoth leads the surge.

Echoes in the Dragon's Lair

In shadows deep, the whispers weave,
Ancient tales that none believe.
Fires flicker, shadows dance,
Echoes call with every glance.

Through the mist, a dragon soars,
Guarding riches behind closed doors.
Claws like daggers, eyes aglow,
Secrets buried, tales of woe.

Voices linger, soft and clear,
In this realm, what do we fear?
With every breath, the magic stirs,
In the air, the dragon purrs.

Time stands still, the heart beats fast,
In the lair, shadows are cast.
Legends whisper, truth concealed,
Dreams of power, fate revealed.

As darkness fades, the dawn breaks near,
Echoes fade, yet still we hear.
The dragon rests, its tales untold,
In the lair, where hearts grow bold.

Enchanted Flutes of the Fiery Keep

In the keep where fires roar,
Flutes enchant with ancient lore.
Melodies that make hearts sigh,
Filling dreams that dance and fly.

Notes like embers, drifting high,
Curling smoke beneath the sky.
Guardians of the fiery night,
Playing tunes of pure delight.

Whispers swirl with passions bold,
Stories of the brave and old.
Each sweet note, a tale to tell,
In the keep where legends dwell.

Crimson flames and golden light,
Guide the dancers through the night.
Flutes of magic, spirits rise,
In this keep, the soul defies.

As dawn approaches, silence reigns,
The flutes rest, yet magic remains.
In the fiery keep's tender groves,
Echoes linger, and love still grows.

Chords of the Celestial Beast

In the night, the stars collide,
A beast awakens, deep inside.
Chords of power weave through the dark,
In the silence, sparks a spark.

Wings like whispers brush the sky,
Celestial calls that never lie.
Each chord thrums with ancient grace,
In this realm, time finds its pace.

The beast's heart beats with cosmic light,
Guiding lost souls through the night.
Harmonies echo, blending sound,
In this dance, all dreams are found.

Voices rise, a seamless blend,
Music flows, it has no end.
With every note, the heavens sigh,
In celestial chords, spirits fly.

As night yields to morning's hue,
The beast retreats, bid adieu.
Chords linger faint, yet still they tease,
In the air, whispers of the breeze.

An Ode in the Smoky Vault

Within the vault, the shadows dwell,
Secrets held, no tongue can tell.
Smoke arises, curling high,
Memories drift, a silent sigh.

In dim light, old treasures gleam,
An ode whispers, like a dream.
Fading echoes, tales of yore,
In the vault, where spirits soar.

Dusty tomes and relics rare,
Breathe the dreams of souls laid bare.
Each page turn, a world awakes,
In smoky trails, the heart aches.

Candles flicker, shadows sway,
A soothing chant, to guide the way.
With every note, the past pays toll,
An ode to time, to every soul.

As silence falls, the night grows deep,
Into the vault, the memories seep.
In smoky whispers, the tale resides,
An ode of hearts, where truth abides.

Melodies of the Hidden Hollow

In the quiet glade where shadows play,
Whispers of secrets dance and sway.
Leaves converse in a gentle breeze,
Nature's symphony, a heart's reprise.

A brook hums softly, a tender song,
Petals flutter, wild and strong.
Each note blends in the twilight's hue,
A melody ancient, pure and true.

Fireflies blink like tiny stars,
Guiding lost souls from afar.
The night embraces with open arms,
Carrying dreams and whispered charms.

Beneath the moon's soft, silver light,
Creatures stir, emerging from night.
They gather 'round in tranquil grace,
Finding solace in this sacred space.

Here in this hollow, time stands still,
Voices echo with the forest's will.
Melodies weave through tree and vine,
A tapestry of life, divine.

Harmonies of the Ancient Flame

In the hearth's glow, stories unfold,
Whispers of legends in embers bold.
Flickering shadows, they cast their spell,
Echoing tales that time will tell.

Beneath the ash, a warmth remains,
Cycle of life in joy and pains.
Each spark a memory, each flame a dream,
Harmonies rise, like a river's gleam.

Voices of ancestors drift through the air,
In the crackle and pop, their spirits share.
Through smoke and fire, their wisdom flows,
Ancient songs that the heart knows.

Gathered around, we feel the pull,
Of distant past, both fierce and full.
In the glow of the flame, we unite,
Lost in the rhythm of the night.

With every flicker, a promise made,
To honor the paths that life has laid.
Together we sit, in silence and light,
Savoring peace in the warmth of the night.

Chronicles of the Celestial Beasts

High above, the stars collide,
Myths awaken, in twilight's tide.
Wings unfurl, bright against the dark,
Celestial beasts ignite their spark.

In constellations, stories weave,
Mysteries mended, secrets believe.
Each creature soars, on currents of fate,
Gliding through the universe's gate.

The lion roars, a king of lore,
While the serpent whispers tales of yore.
Beneath the moon's watchful gaze,
They dance in the night, a cosmic maze.

Phoenix rises from ashes long,
In fiery colors, bold and strong.
Unicorns gallop with grace and flair,
Each step a promise woven in air.

Together they roam, in silence profound,
In realms where magic and dreams abound.
Chronicles written in stardust and light,
A tapestry woven on a canvas of night.

Ballads from the Depths of the Cave

Deep in the dark, where silence reigns,
Whispers echo through stone domains.
Droplets fall in a rhythmic flow,
Secrets hidden, where few dare go.

Stalactites glimmer with ancient might,
Illuminated softly by the moonlight.
The earth's heartbeat resonates low,
In this sacred space, the shadows grow.

Echoes of voices, lost in the fold,
Ballads of time, ages old.
Their stories linger in the chilled air,
Filled with longing, pain, and care.

Gathered around, we listen close,
Tales of the past, what matters most.
The cave sings softly, a haunting tune,
Under the watch of a sullen moon.

In depths we find a stirring spark,
Illuminating truths hidden in the dark.
Ballads resound, a melody brave,
Echos of life from the depths of the cave.

Chronicles of a Whirling Tempest

In the heart of the storm's embrace,
Winds whisper secrets, a wild chase.
Lightning dances, fierce and bright,
Echoes of thunder, slicing the night.

Clouds collide in a furious spin,
Nature's fury, where chaos begins.
Raindrops fall like scattered dreams,
The tempest howls, or so it seems.

Across the sky, a canvas torn,
Colors clash where tempests are born.
A whirlwind's story, ancient and bold,
Tales of courage, waiting to be told.

Through swirling gales, the echoes roam,
Finding solace far from home.
In the eye of a tempest, calm prevails,
Where bravery whispers amidst the gales.

Chronicles written upon the air,
A dance of chaos, wild and rare.
In each gust, a memory spins,
The whirling tempest, where life begins.

Harmony in the Flicker of Tails

Beneath the moon, shadows glide,
Whispers linger, a soft tide.
Tails flicker in the gentle night,
Harmony born from the pale light.

Dancing creatures, a waltz so sweet,
In the stillness, their hearts meet.
Swaying softly, in silent grace,
Nature's chorus, a warm embrace.

Paws touch softly on the dew-kissed ground,
In every heartbeat, a rhythm found.
The flicker of tails, stories to tell,
Woven in moonbeams, casting a spell.

Gentle breezes carry their song,
In the woodland where they belong.
Harmony sings in the quiet air,
A symphony crafted with loving care.

As dawn approaches, shadows blend,
The dance of night, it must end.
Yet in the heart, the music stays,
In flickers of tails, and twilight's haze.

Melodies Carved in Stone

Ancient ruins, stories untold,
Whispers of time in the cold.
Melodies linger where shadows creep,
Echoing secrets the stones keep.

Carved by hands from ages past,
Each groove a moment, forever cast.
In the silence, the songs arise,
Resonating through timeless skies.

Nature's artistry, a sculptor's dream,
Flowing like water, a gentle stream.
Wind caresses the silent walls,
Melodies echo as twilight falls.

Under starlight, the stories play,
Notes of history, here they stay.
In every crack, a tale unfolds,
Of bravery, love, and hearts of gold.

As shadows dance and whispers rhyme,
Melodies carved, transcending time.
In the heart of the stone, they reside,
Resounding softly, a timeless guide.

The Dance of the Firekeeper

In the flickering glow of embers bright,
The firekeeper sways in the night.
With every spark, a story ignites,
A dance with shadows, the heart takes flight.

Wrapped in warmth of the glowing flame,
Ancient whispers call her name.
Twisting and turning, she moves with grace,
In the fire's embrace, she finds her place.

Flames leap high in a spirited dance,
Each flicker an echo, a fleeting chance.
The night listens closely, wrapped in gold,
As the firekeeper's tales unfold.

With every twist, a flicker of fate,
In the dance of warmth, they captivate.
Sparks rise like dreams into the sky,
In their shimmer, the wishes fly.

As dawn breaks, the embers fade,
Yet in her heart, the dance won't jade.
For the firekeeper knows this truth:
In every end, there's a spark of youth.

Whispers of the Fiery Melody

In shadows deep, the embers glow,
Soft whispers rise, like breezes flow.
A spark ignites the fading night,
As flames entwine in ardent flight.

With every note, a story spun,
The fiery dance has just begun.
Alive with passion, hearts will soar,
In rhythmic waves, we crave for more.

The melody, a sweet caress,
In twilight's grasp, we find our rest.
With every breath, a promise made,
Together lost, we are unafraid.

Through swirling smoke, we find our way,
A song of hope that will not sway.
In fiery notes, our spirits wake,
Bound by the love that we both take.

So hold me close, let music rise,
In whispers soft beneath the skies.
Together we will chase the light,
In fiery melody, hearts ignite.

The Enchanted Harmony of Scales

Upon the stage, the scales align,
A symphony of sound divine.
Notes like jewels, brightly soar,
In harmony, we seek for more.

With whispered dreams, the strings will hum,
To ancient tunes, our hearts succumb.
A dance of fingers, swift and bright,
In every touch, the stars ignites.

The woodwinds weave a tender tale,
While brass resounds in bold exhale.
With every beat, a pulse so clear,
United in this magic sphere.

A timeless rhythm guides the way,
In every heart, the music stays.
The scales enchant, we lose our fear,
In harmony, our souls draw near.

Each note bestowed, a gift in sound,
In music's arms, our dreams are found.
The enchanted night will never fade,
In melodies, our love is made.

Echoes from the Cavernous Heart

Deep in the dark, where shadows weave,
Echoes linger, hearts believe.
With every drop, a memory fades,
In cavernous halls, our dreams cascade.

The whispered tales, they shroud the night,
In cavernous depths, we find our light.
With every heartbeat, stories churn,
In silence deep, our passions burn.

A hollow space where secrets lie,
In echoed breaths, we learn to fly.
With every sound, a love will grow,
In cavern's heart, we learn to know.

So venture forth, embrace the call,
In echoed verses, we shall enthrall.
Let every shadow guide our way,
In cavernous heart, we choose to stay.

The whispers fade, but love remains,
In every echo, hope sustains.
From depths profound, our spirits rise,
In cavernous hearts, eternal ties.

Dances in the Dragon's Lair

In dragon's lair, where shadows play,
The flames of fate will lead the way.
With every step, the magic swirls,
As ancient secrets dance and twirl.

Beneath the scales, the heart does beat,
In rhythmic pulse, our souls will meet.
With firelight flickers, the courage blooms,
In dragon's den, our passion looms.

The air is thick with tales untold,
In bravest hearts, a fire bold.
With every leap, a world unfurls,
As we embrace the night that swirls.

In shadows cast, our spirits leap,
In dragon's lair, we sow and reap.
With laughter ringing through the night,
Together we ignite the light.

So take my hand, let's dance anew,
In dragon's embrace, the skies turn blue.
With every moment, our spirits flare,
In vibrant hues, we dance in air.

Serpent's Song: The Legacy of Roars

In shadows deep, the serpent glides,
A whispering roar that never hides.
Ancient echoes stir the night,
Carving stories in moon's light.

Once a king in emerald scales,
Wrapped in legends, whispered tales.
Each flick of tongue, a tale is spun,
Of battles fought and victories won.

The ground trembles with each breath,
Through silent woods, a dance with death.
His legacy, fierce and true,
Awakens dreams for me and you.

Secrets buried in the soil,
Roots entangled in time's coil.
From the earth, his power glows,
Forever bound, the story flows.

Echoes linger, a timeless song,
In the hearts of those who belong.
The serpent's dance, a spiral fate,
Revealing paths, we contemplate.

Strings of the Ancient Dreamer

Beneath the stars, the dreamer sighs,
With fingers strung, he caresses skies.
Whispers of time weave through his tune,
Awakening night, beneath the moon.

Each note a thread, a tale to share,
Of worlds unseen, of love and care.
In harmonic realms, his spirit takes flight,
Crafting visions in the soft twilight.

The ancient wood, it bends and sways,
Resounding stories of forgotten days.
In every pluck, a heartbeat thrums,
A symphony of what becomes.

Fragile moments, they dance and play,
Merging dreams in the dusk's ballet.
The strings may twine, or fray and part,
Yet bind forever within the heart.

As music fades, the echoes cling,
Embracing all that silence brings.
An ancient dreamer, forever bold,
Through melodies, life's tale is told.

The Orchestra of Embered Souls

In twilight's glow, the embers spark,
Soft whispers call out through the dark.
An orchestra of gentle sighs,
With every flicker, a spirit flies.

Strings of sorrow intertwined in fate,
Echoes of laughter, resonate.
Together they dance on the edge of time,
Crafting harmony, pure and sublime.

Flames of longing, rise and fall,
In the heart's embrace, they hear the call.
With every swell, the shadows play,
An ember's glow, lighting the way.

Resilient sparks in the fading light,
Revealing truths hidden from sight.
The orchestra breathes, a timeless tune,
Carving paths in the heart of the moon.

As night descends, the music sways,
Emboldened spirits in endless arrays.
They meld and flow, a fiery swirl,
An orchestra of souls, forever unfurl.

Rhythmic Flight through Starlit Skies

Through endless night, the shadows glide,
On wings of dreams, they gently ride.
In starlit skies, where whispers play,
A rhythmic flight in soft ballet.

With every beat, the cosmos stirs,
A dance unfolds as fate occurs.
The universe hums a gentle song,
Guiding each soul to where they belong.

Galaxies twirl in a ballroom grand,
Elysian pathways hand in hand.
In harmony, they spin and sweep,
Awakening wonders from their sleep.

The pulse of night, alive and bright,
Invites the heart to take its flight.
In rhythmic waves, we lift and soar,
To distant worlds, forevermore.

Beneath the stars, our spirits rise,
We chase the dreams that fill the skies.
Unbound by fate, in endless trails,
Together we weave through starlit sails.

The Dance of Fiery Fables

In twilight's glow, stories ignite,
Whirling flames in the night.
Spirits twirl in fervent plays,
Echoing dreams of ancient days.

With every step, they play their part,
Binding souls with fiery art.
Legends spark in vibrant hue,
A dance of fables, bold and true.

Around the hearth, the tales unfold,
Warriors brave and treasures bold.
Glowing embers, whispers rise,
Secrets wrapped in midnight skies.

In rhythm, they spin, collide,
History's threads, woven with pride.
Forged in flames, each story glows,
In the heart, the adventure flows.

As dawn approaches, shadows retreat,
Fiery fables, bittersweet.
Yet in their wake, a spark remains,
A dance eternal in joy and pains.

Secrets of the Thrumming Wings

Whispers rise on evening's sigh,
Thrumming wings in the sky.
Nature's tune, a soft embrace,
Lives entwined in silent grace.

Within the trees, a secret song,
Echoes of where the heart belongs.
Fluttering, they weave the air,
Tales of journeys, truths laid bare.

Dance of colors, swift and bright,
A fleeting glimpse, a pure delight.
In harmony, they soar and glide,
Chasing dreams without a guide.

Every thrum, a story shared,
In the stillness, hearts prepared.
Secrets whispered with every beat,
Nature's pulse, a soothing treat.

As twilight calls, they take their flight,
Holding close the fading light.
In their wake, the world awakes,
Hope renewed with each breath it takes.

Chasing the Winds of Myth

Across the fields where legends roam,
Mythic whispers call us home.
On windswept paths, we chase the tales,
Through hidden valleys, endless trails.

With every gust, a story drifts,
In shadows where the memory lifts.
Voices echo, inviting, free,
The call of myths, our destiny.

Clouds gather, skies turn gray,
Yet in our hearts, we'll find the way.
Chasing dreams that lift and soar,
Through myths that weave forevermore.

In ancient realms, where spirits play,
We ask for guidance, day by day.
The winds of myth are strong and fierce,
Unraveling truths that time cannot pierce.

As evening falls, the stars align,
A cosmic dance, fate's design.
Chasing shadows, chasing light,
In the winds, our hopes take flight.

The Song of the Embers' Breath

In the hush of twilight's grace,
Embers flicker, softly trace.
Whispers of the fire's glow,
Secrets only night can know.

Each ember sings a gentle tune,
Beneath the watchful silver moon.
The warmth spreads in tender sighs,
A melody that never dies.

As shadows dance with flames entwined,
Stories of the past unwind.
In the heart, a rhythm beats,
The embers' breath, where time repeats.

Flickering sparks like stars above,
Carrying tales of loss and love.
The song weaves through the night's embrace,
An echo of the fires we face.

With every breath, the fire speaks,
A promise found in gentle peaks.
In the silence, we find our way,
Listening close to what they say.

Twirls of the Aether's Song

In the dance of cosmic light,
Stars whisper tales of night.
Winds weave through skies so vast,
Carrying echoes of the past.

Clouds cradle dreams on high,
As they drift and softly sigh.
Notes ripple through the celestial sea,
Painting worlds where spirits flee.

Twirls spin in an endless embrace,
Coloring shadows with their grace.
Galaxies hum a lullaby,
Swirling tunes as starlings fly.

Voices ripple, soft and bright,
In the velvet of the night.
Celestial hands strum the air,
A symphony of dreams laid bare.

Aether sings with whispers sweet,
As time and space elegantly meet.
In twirls of song, we find our way,
Guided by the night's ballet.

Search for the Sonic Gale

Across the fields of echoes wide,
Where melodies and whispers bide,
I seek the wind that sings with might,
A gale of sound that stirs the night.

Mountains hum in deep repose,
A chorus rising where night fields rose.
Veils of sound in shadows weave,
Mysteries that hearts conceive.

Through valleys deep and forests thick,
I chase the notes that dance and flick.
In the pulse of earth, I hear the clue,
A sonic gale calls me, pure and true.

With every breath, I feel its pull,
A rhythm that makes the spirit full.
In the search, I find my place,
In nature's song, a warm embrace.

The winds will carry me far and wide,
To where the hidden melodies abide.
In the search for the hidden gale,
I lose myself, yet will not fail.

Rhythmic Wanderings in the Dragon's Keep

Within the walls of ancient stone,
Dragons rest and dreams are sown.
Rhythms pulse through shadows deep,
Guarding secrets dragons keep.

Wanderers tread on cracked, old ground,
Where echoes of the past resound.
Footsteps dance with fierce delight,
In the realm where day meets night.

In the glow of emerald fire,
Enchanted hearts rise higher.
Songs of ages yet to tell,
In the dragon's lair, all is well.

Whispers twine through caverns wide,
Ancient treasures in shadows hide.
Each beat brings a tale to light,
In rhythmic wanderings, we take flight.

Together here, in fortitude,
We find our strength, a bond renewed.
In the dragon's keep, we roam and weave,
The songs of wonder, hearts believe.

Symphonies of the Crimson Claw

In the heart of dusk's embrace,
Crimson shadows fill the space.
A claw marks paths of ancient lore,
Symphonies echo forevermore.

Fires flicker, warm and bright,
Casting tales into the night.
Rhythmic whispers kiss the air,
Messages linger everywhere.

Within the wild, the beast roams free,
Dancing with the winds, a symphony.
From heights of mountains to valleys low,
The pulse of journeys begins to flow.

Legends carved in twilight's hue,
Resonate with every view.
To the tune of the crimson claw,
A harmony of nature's law.

Together in the shifting time,
We find our voices, pure and prime.
In symphonies that will not fade,
The heartbeats of the wild cascade.

Harmonizing with the Gales of Fury

The tempest roars, wild and free,
Fury dances, a sight to see.
Winds collide, a fierce embrace,
Nature's song through boundless space.

Clouds converge, a shadowed veil,
Lightning strikes, a vibrant trail.
Chaos swings with rhythmic grace,
In the storm, we find our place.

Whispers ride the gusts of might,
Carried forth through day and night.
Echoes clash, then fade away,
Harmonies in disarray.

Yet in the heart, a calm resides,
Beneath the rage, the passion hides.
With every gust, our spirits soar,
Embracing all the gales restore.

The Elixir of Spinning Tales

In twilight's glow, the stories spin,
Ink flows freely, where dreams begin.
Whispers echo through ancient nights,
A journey born from words' delights.

Characters dance on pages wide,
Adventures bloom, our hearts their guide.
Fables weave with threads of truth,
An elixir to restore our youth.

Mysteries linger at every turn,
Lessons learned in the fires that burn.
With every tale, a world unfurls,
Unraveled secrets, hidden pearls.

The storyteller's voice rings clear,
Binding souls, drawing near.
In every word, a spell we weave,
In spinning tales, we dare believe.

Fire and Whispering Echoes

Fires flicker, embers glow bright,
Each crackle holds a hidden right.
Whispers linger in the night air,
Tales of old that hearts still bear.

Flames dance in an endless chase,
Shadows play a wild embrace.
Echoes murmur of what once was,
Firing memories with every buzz.

Thoughts ignite like sparks afire,
With every breath, we feel desire.
Stories blend in the haze of light,
Whispered dreams that take their flight.

Around the blaze, we find our place,
In fire's warmth, a sacred space.
With every flicker, hope is born,
From whispered echoes, dreams adorned.

The Radiance of Vertiginous Flights

Up we soar to dazzling heights,
With wings of hope on vertiginous flights.
The sun awakes to greet our dreams,
In the sky, our spirit beams.

Clouds embrace with tender grace,
We dance on air, a wild chase.
Horizons stretch, where colors blend,
In this realm, our hearts ascend.

Glimmers shine in each daring leap,
The world below, a secret keep.
With every gust, our fears take flight,
In the dance of day and night.

We land anew, with wisdom gained,
From the heights, our souls unchained.
In the breeze, our hopes ignite,
Embracing life in radiant light.

Songs Draped in Shadows and Light

In the twilight where whispers mend,
Shadows dance, and dreams ascend.
A flicker glows in the night's embrace,
Embers of hope, a warm trace.

Voices blend in the dusky air,
Stories linger, secrets laid bare.
Through the darkness, a spark ignites,
Guiding the hearts to new heights.

The moon smiles down, its silver thread,
Weaving tales where fear has fled.
Nature sways to the serenade,
In silence, the melody is made.

Hope and sorrow, entwined as one,
The dance of life has just begun.
In shadows deep, the light will grow,
A song that only the brave will know.

As night surrenders to dawn's soft cure,
The songs remain, steadfast and pure.
In every heart, the rhythm stays,
Echoing through the fleeting days.

The Melody of Ashen Shores

On the shores where ash meets sea,
Waves whisper tales of what used to be.
Each grain tells stories of fire and rain,
A melody born from loss and gain.

Gulls cry out in the misty gray,
Their voices carry the night's decay.
Footsteps echo on the silent sand,
Marked by dreams that slip from hand.

From the depths, the calls arise,
Songs of longing, unseen ties.
The tide brings forth a lover's sigh,
Underneath the endless sky.

A lighthouse stands, a beacon bright,
Guiding souls through the darkest night.
With every rise, the spirits swell,
In the rhythm of waves, they dwell.

Hope unfurls beneath the sun,
Finding strength after the run.
In ashen shores, the heart finds grace,
A newfound love, a warm embrace.

Rhapsody in the Deepest Grotto

In the grotto where echoes fade,
Whispers of magic softly invade.
Dripping water sings a tune,
A symphony cradled by the moon.

Bats flutter in the cool, dark air,
Notes of dusk weave without a care.
Shadows twist to a phantom beat,
As ancient tales find their seat.

Crystals glimmer with a ghostly light,
Dancing echoes in the heart of night.
Each sound a secret, softly spun,
In the embrace of the hidden one.

Time stands still in the cavern's hold,
A rhapsody rich, a story told.
With every breath, the spirit sings,
Of forgotten lore and hidden things.

In the depths, the world seems far,
Guided gently by the guiding star.
Here, beneath the stony dome,
The heart finds solace, the soul finds home.

The Firesong's Ethereal Echo

In the heart of night, a fire burns bright,
Casting shadows that dance with delight.
The flames sing songs of a time gone by,
Whispers of love beneath the sky.

Each flicker speaks of dreams fulfilled,
Of laughter shared, and spirits thrilled.
Embers soar like wishes released,
In the warmth of a gathering feast.

Crisp air hums with a tender tune,
Melodies rise beneath the moon.
A chorus of voices, sweet and strong,
Together they wove the night's song.

Songs of struggle, passion, and grace,
A rhythmic pulse, an eternal chase.
As shadows weave through the flame's embrace,
The firesong echoes, time can't erase.

In the stillness, hearts beat bright,
Unified under the starlit light.
The legacy lingers, a thread that binds,
In the firesong's echo, a love that finds.

A Symphony of Seething Breath

In shadows deep where silence lies,
A breath ignites the starlit skies.
Each note a whisper in the night,
A symphony of silent light.

The winds of change begin to soar,
With every pulse, I crave for more.
The rhythm dances in the dark,
A fire ignited by a spark.

Beneath the moon's soft silver glare,
I feel the world, a gentle flare.
Each heartbeat echoes distant calls,
As time and space begin to fall.

The quiet notes that swell and rise,
Entwine like vines that touch the skies.
With every breath, a story spun,
A symphony, we are as one.

In seething depths, the sound does swell,
A timeless echo, all is well.
Together lost in harmony,
A breath, a note, eternity.

Whispers and Rhythms of the Flame

In flickered light, the shadows dance,
Whispers carried in a glance.
The flames can tell of ancient past,
Of dreams entwined, forever cast.

Each ember glows with secrets shared,
A warmth that wrapped those who dared.
The rhythm of the fire's glow,
A tale of life, a steady flow.

With every crackle, stories rise,
Of lost loves, battles, heartrending sighs.
The pulse of flame, a beating heart,
In fragile moments, we won't part.

Around the fire, we unite,
In whispers softly—through the night.
The warmth surrounds, the shadows weave,
A tapestry of what we believe.

In fiery tongues, the truth is named,
And in its warmth, we're all reclaimed.
These whispers, rhythms intertwined,
A flame that links the heart and mind.

Tuning the Celestial Spheres

In cradles of the cosmic tune,
The planets hum a mystic rune.
With every twirl, the stardust sings,
A melody of cosmic things.

In boundless space, the echoes play,
From night to dawn, they find their way.
A symphony of orbs and light,
Each note a dance through starry night.

Galaxies swirl in brilliant hues,
The universe whispers its daily views.
In harmony, they spin and glide,
With every note, we feel the tide.

Tuning hearts to celestial sounds,
Uniting souls as laughter bounds.
For in the skies, our spirits touch,
A boundless song, we crave so much.

In cosmic silence, time stands still,
As starlit dreams begin to thrill.
The spheres align, the tune inspires,
In every heart, celestial fires.

Threads of Harmony Under Dragon's Wing

Beneath the shadow of ancient flight,
A dragon glides with grace and might.
Its wings extend like woven dreams,
Where every thread of magic gleams.

In twilight's glow, we find our song,
The threads of fate entwined and strong.
A tapestry of dreams in flight,
Each color glowing in the night.

The whispers rise in soft refrain,
As stars awaken, free from bane.
The dragon sings of moments past,
In harmony, our fates are cast.

Under the wing of mighty grace,
We search for peace, a sacred place.
Each thread a path, a gentle tie,
To spirits soaring through the sky.

In every flicker, shadows weave,
A promise held in hearts that believe.
Through dragon's flight, we soar anew,
In threads of harmony, we grew.

The Faerie's Dance in the Hearth

In the glow where embers play,
Whispers weave through shadows sway.
Tiny feet on twinkling ground,
Faeries twirl without a sound.

Glistening dust, a sparkling trance,
In the firelight, they dance and prance.
Joyful laughter fills the air,
As magic spins both light and care.

With every flicker, stories told,
Of ancient wonders, bright and bold.
Curly wisps of dreams take flight,
In the hearth's enchanting light.

From gentle sways to leaps and bounds,
Softly stirring heartbeats sound.
The night enfolds, the warmth bestows,
The faerie's dance forever glows.

So gather near, embrace the gleam,
Let your spirit drift and dream.
For in this magic, hearts will meet,
At the hearth where faeries greet.

Firelight Rhythms of the Olden Tales

A crackling hearth, a nighttime chill,
Olden tales begin to thrill.
Like flames that rise and dart, they weave,
Stories made to make us believe.

Shadows stretch along the wall,
Echoes of the past enthrall.
With each pop and with each sigh,
Legends wake as sparks pass by.

Voices soft like a hushed embrace,
Kindled memories we can trace.
From dragons bold to lovers lost,
Each fable tells a bittersweet cost.

The warmth surrounds, a protective cloak,
From fiery words, the heart awoke.
In every line and every rhyme,
We find our place in the folds of time.

So let us sit, let stories flow,
Through firelight, we come to know.
The rhythms of our ancestors' tune,
Under the watchful, glowing moon.

Syncopation of Celestial Spirits

Stars align in rhythmic grace,
Celestial spirits take their place.
With pulsating beats that never cease,
They dance through night, a cosmic peace.

Galaxies swirl in vibrant hues,
A melody born of ancient views.
Harmony weaves through heaven's dome,
In the universe, they call it home.

Nebulas glow like a painter's brush,
Creating whispers in the galactic hush.
Each blink of light, a note in time,
Syncopated stardust, a perfect rhyme.

Waves of color, light unfurled,
In this magic, we find our world.
Let the heart beat with the stars above,
In the dance, we feel the love.

So gaze up high, let your spirit soar,
Join the dance, forevermore.
For in each twinkle, dreams take flight,
In syncopation, through the night.

The Thrum of Flames and Legends

The flames, they thrum with stories old,
Of heroes brave and treasures bold.
Whispers rise with flickering light,
In the shadows of the night.

Every crackle, a secret shared,
Of trials faced and hearts that dared.
Legends live where embers die,
Echoing deep in the night sky.

Ashen trails of forgotten lore,
In the hearth, we ask for more.
With every blaze, a spark ignites,
Awakening long-lost delights.

Wrapped in warmth, we weave our dreams,
In the thrum, the fire gleams.
A circle formed, with hands entwined,
Through flames of old, the past we find.

The stories burn, though time may fade,
In the heart of fire, they're forever laid.
So gather 'round, let voices rise,
In the thrum of flames, our spirit flies.

Wails of the Mystic Serpent

In the depths of the night, they moan,
Echoes of secrets, ancient and grown.
Twisting shadows glide with a sigh,
Serpentine whispers beneath the sky.

Flickering candles cast ghostly light,
Guardians of tales in the heart of the night.
Eyes that shimmer with the tales of old,
Wails of the mystics, both haunting and bold.

Riddles entwined in the silken threads,
Crimson and emerald where the darkness spreads.
Slithering visions that dance with grace,
The serpent's allure, a timeless embrace.

Ancient trees cradle the paths long lost,
Every whisper recalls the cost.
In twilight's embrace, shadows conspire,
Wails that awaken forgotten desire.

From the moonlit depths, she beckons the brave,
A journey unspooled from the cradle to grave.
Each cry a promise, each sigh a plea,
In the arms of the serpent, we yearn to be free.

Lullabies of the Golden Treasure

In a cradle of gold, dreams take flight,
Soft as the dawn, gentle as night.
Whispers of riches in shimmering tones,
Lullabies woven from warm-hearted stones.

Waves of the sea hum a melodic plea,
Serenading souls who wander carefree.
Secrets of fortune beneath the sands,
In the embrace of time, clasping our hands.

Stars twinkle softly in twilight's embrace,
Guiding our hearts to a mystical place.
Where laughter sparkles and shadows retreat,
Lullabies linger, a rhythmic heartbeat.

With each gentle breath and a tender sigh,
Golden threads weave through the sky.
Hopes and dreams held in shimmering rays,
Lullabies whisper of brighter days.

In the arms of the night, we drift and sway,
Wrapped in the warmth of gold's soft array.
Forever enchanted by treasure untold,
Lullabies echo as our stories unfold.

Vibrations of the Draconic Spirit

In the realm where legends are spun,
Draconic spirits breathe, a race to run.
With fiery hearts and shimmering scales,
They rise from the depths, igniting the tales.

Echoes of thunder in the skies collide,
Vibrations awaken, no place to hide.
Wings spread wide, like shadows they glide,
Guardians of wisdom in the night, they bide.

Whispers of power through valleys and peaks,
A language of thunder, the mountain speaks.
Breaths of the ancients spill forth with grace,
Vibrations of dreams across time and space.

With every heartbeat, the ground shakes in tune,
Awakening wonders beneath the bright moon.
In flames and in frost, they dance and they sway,
Draconic spirits lead us away.

Through the echoes of now and the whispers of fate,
In the shadows of dawn, we elevate.
For in the dread silence, the draconic inspire,
Vibrations of magic, igniting the fire.

Cadence Beneath the Starlit Wing

In the hush of night, a melody breathes,
Cadence of wonders in twilight weaves.
Beneath the wings that flutter and soar,
Songs of the cosmos, forevermore.

Stars shimmer down with a delicate hum,
Whispers of dreams through the darkness come.
Each glimmer a tale from the ages past,
Cadence in silence, a spell to cast.

Among the clouds where the shadows play,
Magic awakens in a radiant ballet.
The night dances softly, cradled in song,
As starlit wings guide us ever along.

With every note, a heartbeat sings true,
A symphony crafted from night's wondrous hue.
In the weave of the cosmos, spirits align,
Cadence and starlight, a rhythm divine.

In the embrace of the night, we are one,
Tracing the paths where the mysteries run.
Beneath starlit wings, our essence takes flight,
In a cadence of love that conquers the night.

Strains of the Forgotten Realm

In twilight shadows where whispers flow,
Lost stories linger, woven slow.
Echoed footsteps on ancient ground,
Time's soft ballet, a ghostly sound.

Through forests deep, where memories fade,
The breeze carries tunes, a serenade.
Each note a secret, a tale unseen,
Of heroes forgotten, and places serene.

Amidst the ruins, the past ignites,
A symphony sweet in the quiet nights.
With every sigh from the crumbled stone,
The heart of the realm calls us home.

In the stillness, the echoes rise,
Revealing the truth beneath the skies.
A melody played on the strings of time,
In this forgotten realm, all is sublime.

Echoing Laughter of Scale and Flame

In caverns deep where shadows leap,
Dragons laugh as the fires sweep.
Scales that shimmer, eyes aglow,
A dance of passion, a fiery show.

With wings that whisper on the breeze,
Hearts ignite with ancient ease.
Every roar, a spark of glee,
Scaling heights, wild and free.

Laughter echoes through the night,
Crafting tales with sheer delight.
The rhythm of flames, a vibrant hymn,
In the world of scale, where spirits swim.

Boundless joy in a waltz so wild,
The flame-touched creatures, nature's child.
Each jest a flicker; each chuckle a blaze,
An endless dance in a fiery maze.

The Raucous Choir of Fiery Fables

Under the stars where legends dwell,
A choir sings from the mountains' swell.
With voices rich and tales so bold,
Fables of fire, and fortunes untold.

The flames crackle, the stories unfold,
Of lost kingdoms and treasures of gold.
An orchestra made from the night's embrace,
A symphony born of time and space.

Each note ignites the heart with cheer,
Raucous joy in the atmosphere.
Their magic dances on the air,
Whispers of wonder igniting the scare.

With fervent passion, the stories bloom,
Spreading warmth in the lingering gloom.
A feast for the soul, the audience sways,
In the heart of the night, the choir plays.

Whirlwind Verses of the Sky Ruler

Above the clouds where the winds entwine,
The Sky Ruler crafts with a hand divine.
Verses swirl in a tempest's flight,
Dancing clouds, a canvas of light.

A symphony played on a silver string,
Whispers of thunder, the freedom they bring.
Each gust of wind, a lyric so pure,
In the heart of the storm, we endure.

Galaxies spin, and shadows sway,
Caught in the melody of night and day.
The whirlwind sings of journeys grand,
Tracing the dreams drawn in the sand.

With every heartbeat, nature can soar,
The Sky Ruler sings, forevermore.
Verses of wonder blown through the skies,
A testament where the spirit flies.

9 781805 593591